Hand in Hand

HAND IN HAND

Poets Respond to Race

EDITED BY

AL BLACK AND LEN LAWSON

MUDDY FORD PRESS

CHAPIN, SOUTH CAROLINA

MuddyFordPress.com

Library of Congress Number:2017901290

ISBN: 978-1-942081-09-8

The previously published poems of honoree Jeffers, Len Lawson, and Marjory Wentworth appear courtesy of the authors.

Cover art by Kara Gunter
handsoncolumbia.wordpress.com

"My identity might begin with the fact of my race, but it didn't, couldn't end there.
At least that's what I would choose to believe."

— Barack Obama, *Dreams from My Father: A Story of Race and Inheritance*

Contents

Trying to write an introduction is a difficult assignment for me. I have always been the rebellious student who questioned first and sometimes, just refused to do an assignment and would defiantly accept the consequences. If Facebook was around when I was a student, I would be the subject of many a late night post by my professors. I will approach this from why I decided to co-found the 'Poets Respond to Race Initiative' with my friend Len Lawson.

Since high school I have always worked on issues of justice: race, Vietnam War, poverty, literacy, etc. ... as time passed, some issues receded or even disappeared, but the pervasiveness of racism has persisted. Over the years, I have been arrested for agitating and demonstrating for civil rights, I was the Vice President of my local NAACP chapter and a national delegate, a certified diversity trainer for Purdue University, founder of the Race Unity Coalition (a positive response to a Klan rally in Lafayette, IN), to mention a few positions and I have tried to be aware of and take purposeful action to recognize and respond to issues of diversity in the workplace, my community and what I participate in. As I became involved in poetry in South Carolina I purposely attempted to place issues of diversity in the forefront of how I organized events.

The idea of forming an initiative for using poetry as a platform for encouraging dialogues on race in a meaningful way had been swirling about my brain for a while, but I wanted an accomplished written poet to collaborate with, because using a poet who did only spoken word would exclude us from doing bookstores and made us less appealing to schools. Len Lawson was an English instructor at Morris College when my wife introduced us. In late 2014, Len did a poetry feature at a weekly poetry venue I host; when he read, I found out that he had published a book of poetry. I approached him with my concept and we launched our first event in May of 2015.

It has been an interesting ride ever since; in many ways we are polar opposites. Len frustrates the hell out of me with his attention to detail and planning and I infuriate him with my, Alfred E. Newman, "What, me worry?" approach, that is a tad rebellious of convention and purposely does not want to plan so much that form gets in the way of my responding to the moment.

We are good for each other and stronger for it. This anthology is more the vision of Len; I invited po- ets and argued against making it too academic, but the heavy lifting and format is Len's work. Left to me, it would be another great idea left half-finished among my pile of other half-finished great ideas lying on my desk. I also want to acknowledge that this book was the idea of my publisher, Muddy Ford Press; thank you, Cindi Boiter, for hav- ing faith in the vision of 'Poets Respond to Race Initiative.' Worry is the misappropriation of the imagination.

Al Black

alblackblog.com

January 2017

I am a South Carolina native and have lived in the state my entire life. Growing up in the South, I learned that people are not just their skin tones, but they are a combination of what they have been taught (or exposed to) and what they believe. Although I grew up in a desegregated environment, the echoes of the segregated South rung in my home town even nearing the turn of the century. This should be no surprise to anyone. However, I decided as early as my senior year of high school that I would not let those chilling echoes define me as a citizen or as a man.

I am fortunate not to have encountered racism face to face in my life in the South until one recent incident where a white man in Camden, SC, told me to "act like you got some sense" after I needed help getting my broken down vehicle to the side of the road. No, I did not thank him for his assistance. This incident happened a few years after meeting my friend Al Black at his open mic venue Mind Gravy in Columbia, SC. His wife Carol and I taught at the same college at the time, and she thought I should get to know her husband. I found that Al is nothing of what he appears to be. A white man dressed in bohemian button shirts and crocs could give some the wrong impression. Nonetheless, the man's heart for the arts, social justice, and his writing shine through the dubious outfits.

It is this heart of his that approached me about doing a tour where we each read poems and after discuss relevant issues of race in local settings. At first, I balked at the idea out of lack of confidence in my own craft. Al could have chosen a number of more experienced poets to partner with and ones with which he was more familiar (we were not truly friends at the time). I began this journey with him because I wanted to insert my drop in the bucket of activism and to help people of different backgrounds to understand other races whom they encounter daily but either tear down in private or simply ignore altogether.

In the first few tour events, it became less about both of us and more about communities we visited sharing their own truths with a wealth of historical context about the South on the side. I learn much from our audiences rather than trying to educate the masses myself. I go in with an open mind to understand how each venue in each moment can contribute to preventing the next Trayvon Martin or Michael Brown.

We have not always encountered peace in our meetings on the road. We have ruffled the feathers of a few staunch confeder-ates, young men who as I mentioned were born into or taught their heritage. The fact that our words have penetrated their souls to respond by speaking with us privately instead of burn-ing or shooting a church has been remarkable within itself. This is why we continue the tours after initially committing only to one year.

Al and I embrace our role of using arts and activism to pro-mote change in our communities. Incidents like the man in Camden fuel our discussions about how we should approach our events, what issues we should address, and what poets and activists we should collaborate with.

I am happy to present the contributors who have agreed to submit their work by our invitation. This work would not be possible without their selfless art and willing spirits. I am humbled to have work by such accomplished poets as South Carolina Poet Laureate Marjorie Wentworth and the outstand-ing Honoree Jeffers as well as emerging dynamos like Cortney Lamar Charleston and Tiana Clark.

Al and I do not seek to be our own dynamic duo fighting for justice on our own. We realize it takes a community of voices to establish a gateway toward the tough conversations about race and racism.

My personal goal for this project is that it reaches young, aspiring writers and activists who have a similar fire inside them for change in their communities and the world. I want them to see that, yes, they can inspire others with their words and, yes, other people will read and listen to their message. I want them to learn from elders past and present who have gone before them paving the way for their understanding and their success. With this anthology, so many voices can reach farther than Al and I could alone to show the next generation of arts activists the power of unity with the community.

I want to thank Ed Madden and Cindi Boiter for their patience and vision with this project. The Jasper Project continues to be the heartbeat of South Carolina Midlands literary, musical, theatrical, and visual arts.

Finally, to my partner, my friend, Al Black, thank you for acting on what you saw in this young black man trying to discover his voice in the world. You continue to teach me through your knowledge and wisdom not only about poetry but about manhood. You are not just an associate. You have become a lifelong friend. God bless you, and may God bless all who encounter these poems.

Len Lawson

January 2017

Dasan Ahanu

Wilted Flowers

for lost young lives

My grandmother loved to tell people
about the features
she credited to the Cherokee
in her lineage
and not my father
Learnt me that the legacy
is more important than those
responsible

When the next young black tomorrow
is laid in a casket
What features will be claimed?
Will the streets,
activists,
newspapers
claim that the legacy
is more important
than those responsible?

Martyrdom has become
the new puberty
Adolescence is a ticking time bomb
seen as black terrorism
Uniformed response
is deemed fatal heroism
by jury boxes with no tongue
and no backbone

Don't hold toy guns baby boy
Don't hold a belief that arrival
will mean order baby girl

Don't move
Don't breath
Don't hope
Don't be
Contractions are abbreviated life spans
delivered by reapers
who relish
for moments to touch darkness
and manipulate it quiet

Since when were siblings supposed to
say goodbye to little brother
making pilgrimage to pearly gates
in their arms?
Since when are we supposed to
get used to
flowers bedded in asphalt
becoming pollinated
by the bumble bee of gunshots?

There is reason
to attack the present from all sides
until the future submits to our will
The past is filled with premature obituaries
Respectability is an improper eulogy
Ain't no need to sanitize our culture
They been wiping our blood off of concrete
The smell of bleach
is the new mistress to the dawn's sun
White out used to be the appropriate
tool to erase the presence of black ink
Now white media

is the preferred tool to negate the
humanity of black names
This here be a call for an organized
and strategic awakening
Oppression
is a brown thumbed gardener
tending to communities disregarded
by the city's fungal sense
of fiduciary responsibility
Shock transplanted in media outlets
Flowers cut down
before their purpose sees fruition
Concern waterlogging
the shoulders of blossoming buds
gathered in a protective motherly embrace
Too little light shined
on predatory or prejudiced
practices

There is no beautiful planned
for these blessings to flourish and grow
The flowers
The flowers
They wilt

Marcus Amaker

Mahogany

Who decided to call us "black and white"?
When I look at my skin,
I don't see black,
I see brown.

Brown. Like the color of sand,
a brilliant tan that needs no sun.
Brown, like the mahogany tree bark,
grounded in the summer,
whose green leaves make the transition into fall,
coffee-stained by the autumn's cool breeze.

Who decided to call us "black and white"?
When I look at my wife,
I don't see white,
I see brown.
Just a lighter shade
than mine.

Brown is the cinnamon
that colors her iris.
Brown are the arms
that wrap around me
during a bronze sunset.
Brown are the layered bricks
of our home's
foundation.

Who decided to call us "black and white"?
When I look at all of you,
I see shades of brown.

A sea of one color.
Ripples of love
floating along a sea change.

There are so many words used to divide us.
To fool us into seeing ourselves
through foggy lenses.

We are more
than a box-checked statistic,
we are more
than a census.
I am not black
or white.

I am awake.

Jennifer Bartell

Amazing, That Grace

after Mother Emmanuel AME
Rev. Clementa Pickney's
funeral processional
is coming through the small
town in which I was raised.

We are all lined up on the sidewalks,
white and black, waving small American flags.
Showing our solidarity with the family,
with Mother Emmanuel,
with Charleston, with the nation,
with the world.

We look down the road and wait for
Rev. Clementa Pickney.

I was driving when I heard the eulogy,
when I heard our first black president
singing "Amazing Grace."

And I remember how "Amazing
Grace" was written on board
a slave ship, how thousands of Africans
brought to America came
through the port of Charleston.

Now Rev. Clementa Pickney
is making his way to his final port,
a graveyard in Marion.

We look down the road,
waiting.
It's just awful
what happened, it's just awful,
a white woman says with tears
in her eyes. I can only shake my
head, not wanting to speak
any tears out my own eyes.

How amazing that grace is to see
his family with windows down
waving to us on that hot
sidewalk in June. I feel the
love coming off of their hands.
Their faces amazed to see so many
of us in so many of these small
towns on the road from
Charleston to Marion,
ushering them into port like
little lighthouses lighting the path.

The tears rush out of my body
like the river running to the sea.

Al Black

For the Poet, Ashraf Fayadh*

Tell my mother
I'll be home late
Tell my lover
eight years is too long
to wait for human touch
Tell my father
I will survive
Tell the pious
I have a photo booth
hidden deep inside
where I will take selfies
that they will not find
Tell them all
when I am released
I will let them read the poems
they carved into my back

*Ashraf Fayadh is a Palestinian poet. Recently, while in Saudi Arabia, he posted to social media a selfie of himself standing next to women friends at an art gallery without them being veiled. He was arrested by religious authorities and tried for the selfie and poems of his that had been published some years ago in another country. They sentenced him to death by beheading; international outcry forced them to retry him. This time he was again found guilty in religious courts and sentenced to 8 years in prison and 1,000 lashes.

It Lingers

This morning, watching mist rise off the lake
No wind, the water is motionless
Clouds float above my face in a liquid mirror
I am an interloper and a voyeur
Someone who does not belong here
O' the air hangs heavy over the 'Land of Cotton'
It lingers in the streets, in the fields
In the air above still water

I was born on the banks of the Wabash
Where winds blow hard
Coming down off the Great Lakes
Like a speeding semi out of Chicago
Barreling over the plains of the Calumet
Heading south on I65 towards Indianapolis
Winds that build snow drifts in the winter
Winds that change the seasons
Winds that cool the summer heat

Yesterday, my wife came home from college
She had given a lecture on racial identity
Showing a series of photographs of people
She asked students to identify race
Some were of our grandchildren
A white student apologized for calling them black
A black student asked if she went
Out in public with our grandchildren
. . . a culture still shackled . . .
O' the air hangs heavy over the 'Land of Cotton'
It lingers in the streets, in the fields
In the air above still water

Blood

Blood upon the jungle floor — blood upon the Kings of
Ghana
Blood upon the deck of ships — blood upon the sea
Blood upon the auction block — blood upon the shackles
Blood upon the cotton bales stacked high in Charleston Bay

Blood upon the ramparts — blood upon the bayonets
Blood upon Antietam fields – blood upon the swords of
wrath
Blood upon 600,000 graves – blood upon the rebel flag
Blood upon a band that plays sweet Dixie Land

Blood upon old money — blood upon a crow named Jim
Blood upon white sheets – blood upon a hangman's noose
Blood upon a billy club – blood upon a hotel balcony
Blood upon this nation – blood upon you and me

Gil Scott Heron Revisited

The revolution will be televised
it will be on youtube, google and facebook
brought to you by 10,000 smart phones

The revolution will be televised
no one will lead the charge
it will just spontaneously combust

The revolution will be televised
Beiber and Taylor will not be singing
but Kylie will be posting selfies

The revolution will be televised
on laptops, ipads and tablets
and when it is over, Kanye will still grab the mic

The revolution will be televised
cameras reveal the truth
police lies no longer work

The revolution will be televised
The revolution is being televised
We all are being televised.............

After The Flag

Tell me, brother
of our ancient brown-skinned mother
how ocean carnivores gathered
along the middle passage
and feasted upon the dead
sing to me
of the bones of souls
that line the ocean floor
pointing the way home
dance with me
along historic streets
entertaining wealthy tourists
who dine on recycled human protein
they called lobster, shrimp and catch of the day
and ask them to explain why
after the mother church massacre
after all the rallies and marches
after legislators confessed their guilt
after the flag came down
black churches still burn across the South

1960's Small Town Indiana Blues

On Saturday mornings
we would hang out
but only after we
picked up trash from your yard
because black folk weren't supposed
to move above the hill

When you rode the Ferris wheel
with a girl who liked you
her dad and brother
beat her black and blue
because white girls don't sit
on carnival rides with black boys

When I made you go with me
to get my haircut
the old black man who sat quietly
by the shoe shine chair
in the back of the shop
motioned me out the back door
when I was done

There you sat in the alley
by the trash cans
eyes closed
back against the wall
your grandfather told me
black boys aren't allowed
in barber shops on Main Street
if they want to shine shoes

Hand in Hand

50 years later
in front of the fire station
little cast iron black boys
no longer obediently hold lanterns
for little cast iron white boys
but I listen to the election news
and still get those 1960's small town Indiana Blues
and think maybe Martin was wrong
and brother Malcolm was right

Bernard Block

Black Is the Color...

after Roxanne Gay
for Sandra Bland

I am Sandra Bland
I do not feel alive
I feel like I am not dead yet
I hang on a wire in Ravenwood Jail
          in Waller County, Texas
Stripped of my unruly black body

I was stopped on the black-top
          of Highway 29 by Police Officer Encinia
It was black twilight   I was driving while black
Mr. Encinia asked why I was irritated
I answered the question I was asked
Mr. Encinia did not like my tone
          it was black
Mr. Encinia told me to put my cigarette out
          I refused
He threatened to light up my black body
          with his Taser
I was pulled from my black car
          in black twilight
I protested   placed in black handcuffs
I stated my black rights

$5,000 bail where was I gonna' get 5,000 black dollars
According to the Autopsy Report
I am hanging on a black wire
In Ravenwood County Jail   in Waller County, Texas
          Stripped of my unruly black body

25

Kim Blum- Hyclak

Excerpt from "In the Absence of Color"

Part II

Standing room only at the Soul-Food Cook-off.
Suits and scrubs, jeans and shorts, Black and white,
young and old. Hip-hop music keeps us bouncing
on our toes, draws a little white girl to the center
releasing through her arms and legs the rhythm in her heart.
Our plates piled high with spicy hoppin' john, dark green
collards, crispy hog jowls like thick strips of bacon, short ribs,
corn bread and sweet potato pone. Fried pickles
still bright green under tan batter, fried okra and fried
chicken, creamy mac-n-cheese, creamy red-skinned potato
salad. Red beans and rice in gravy, shrimp swimming in
herbed butter. Banana pudding, peach cobbler and cold
peach soup. At our table of eight the comparisons begin
Now my momma fixes her greens like this...'
We exchange names we'll never remember,
probably never see each other again. At our table of eight
I'm the only one absent of color.

Roger Bonair-Agard

Excerpt from the Elegba interviews / treatise /

or… what next now Papa Legba?

1.
Subplot

Maybe I can tend to the garden
again. Wield machete and hoe, bust
through the earth that eventually forgives.
A man is still most alive by the sweat
his body can make of its own work
until the very self leaves the self as salt
returning to the dirt.

Maybe this is how to make the body
study now, steady now. Build a new
discipline or re-tool an old one that
can sustain the body which houses the fickle
brain and quiets the noisy and restless imps
weaving their everlasting quilts of blood
and self-harm and worthlessness and doubt.

Isn't it after all that the body knows itself
and its limits after a night of dancing? Isn't
the night closing in on the body at all times
except when it moves to push its dark

walls back? What to name the new vigor
my body is about to birth? What is my work
now that I've reproduced myself?

Call me plough. Call me gravedigger.

Call me road grader. Call me scout.
Call me he who makes a way. Call me
he who avoids the bullet. Call me he
who takes it so she won't have to. Call
me bullet-proof. Call me resurrect.
Call me never-dead. Call me Greatest
Of All Time. Call me prophet. Call
me by my name. Call me father. Call
me citizen. Call me vine, blade
and the sinews that swing it. Call me
the weave pattern of resist itself.
Call me revolt.

2.
Situation

Someone is burning black churches.
Someone is setting fire to blackness
in the night and watching it be ash
by morning. In the dream, the man
waves me down on the highway to ask
what A.M.E. means. I tell him
and immediately regret. The most American
thing we have learned is how to plunder
and pretend our robbery was our victim's
salvation. In the dream I'm the man
on the roadside too. Call me he who
builds a church in the night. Call me
he who sets it ablaze.

3.
Soapbox

The movement needs two kinds of soldier
Builders and burners. Praise the hands that
set the CVS alight. Praise the looters

like ants scurrying from the Quik Trip.
Praise the man in the photo with the bandanna
mask. Praise the boy who returns the live teargas
canister to the bewildered police. Praise black
bodies always running. Praise the dream defenders
Praise Netta. Praise Deray. Praise Ta-Nehesi. Praise
New York City. Praise Bree Newsome. Praise
Ferguson and Los Angeles and Staten Island
and Charleston and Baltimore. Praise the flag
that is a burning corporation. Praise the black flag.
Praise guns in the hood waiting to clap back
at the right time. Praise the right time. It is
the right time. We are the right time.

4.

Etymology

This is how to make the body study now,
steady now, sturdy now, stealthy now. Build
with all the tools. Be the discipline, disciple,
decisive, deceptive. Be sod turner and seed planter.
Be path clearer and the hand that knows to lift
the bird's nest down before the blade cleaves
the perfect arc. Be the perfect arc and comeback.
Be the body willing to burn. Be the celebration
dance. Be the muscles pushing themselves
against the walled darkness. Be the night
itself when the riders come. Be the blood
and the vigor, the vigilance, the violence.
Be the rigor, the regal, the rage. Be the garden
the Eden, the powerful, the evil
the growth, the knowledge, the place to return to.
Be the morning and the clear sky insisting - begin
again. Be the mourning, even when yours is the finger
on the trigger, the hand on the heavy hilt.

5.

These three things
Be alive
Be black
Burn. Build.

Fran Cardwell

Son of the Confederacy As Seen on the Noon News

I saw him say it on TV,
that son of the Confederacy,
as he stood in front of the monument
beneath his flag,
"The killer wants to start a race war.
We'll give him what he wished for.
This is war."
I heard him say it,
but could not believe my ears.
Eight days earlier,
I saw on TV
the killer as he listened to the families
forgive him nine times.
How difficult it must have been for them,
how against human nature,
how it must have taken every bit of faith
in the teachings of their Jesus
they could summon up
out of their hurting hearts.
With their words they started a conversation
of love heard round the world.
They and we are all the richer for it.
That man at the monument,
there are no words sufficient
to describe his poverty of spirit.

Cortney Lamar Charleston

I Said, "Give Me Liberty, or Give Me Death"

and they tried to give me death.   *It was all rather predictable.*

　　　The stats don't lie because they don't actually speak.

I hear the dead and see the people that killed them on TV,

doing interviews.　　　God refuses to answer my questions.

　　　The safest I feel inside a church is at my own funeral.

My body is always in mourning.　　　I walk into the night
and

disappear.　　　They're out looking for me because

I fit a description.　　　Somehow, I spend my whole life in
prison

but was never even alive.　　　I call a stillborn nation home.

Tiana Clark

Formal Rage

for Freddie Gray

If we must die, let it not be like hogs
Hunted and penned in an inglorious spot
Claude McKay

Lead chips and petals of paint from your home,
your death began with heavy metal, the wardrobe
of Nessus poisoned your blood and bone.
Your body, sacrament to the pyre in Baltimore.
Gray as volcanic smoke uprising the wolf.
Ashen cross on your forehead: you are dust
and to dust you shall return. Oh gray—gulf
between black/white and the knife in your just
pocket. The storm flood grays as your shackled
body bobs in the back of a police van—breaking
spine to shattered glass—gray wreckage of culled
liquids, dying stain pressed to the floor. Shout
we shall overcome for you, charge depravity
of hearts—beating fists as gray chants to thee.

Julia Dawson

Dear Black Woman

What can my spirit
born to this light skin
say to yours in your
dark, first-mother form
in this place
now called
America?

At first, I stutter, stumble.

There's no place I
white woman
can stand,
to say a thing to you
black woman

unless it starts with:

I have betrayed you.

When I sat silent as
my father left England's shores
trading guns and horses
for your family

When my husband
built fortunes from your labor
in Carolina rice fields
poisoned days with
child-sized hand cuffs and
beds bloodied by rape

When, on Alabama sharecrop farms
I kept the books for Daddy
watched him lie to yours on settling day.
Heard your Daddy challenge the math,
then saw how quickly he was gone;
noted the charred skin on Daddy's cattle rope
but said nothing

When—1955, near Money, Mississippi—
I lied about your fourteen-year-old son
to a county judge
said he grabbed me by the waist, lustful

When today I leave white flight suburbs
to buy homes on city blocks
I wouldn't visit before your friends were pushed out

When I go shopping again
instead of paying attention
to the demonstration you organized
to keep your neighborhood intact

When I later welcome you
to that same neighborhood
then become offended when you
do not thank me

When I refuse to question
the history we were both taught
and tell my college-aged sons
We have, because we earned it

When today I play "cool parent"
allow keg parties and pot
Then don't listen
(because it makes me uncomfortable)
as you

black mother
ask why your children are
jailed, watched, trailed, stopped, frisked,
given chokeholds instead of respect
by secret shoppers, police,
school resource officers
for the same acts or nothing at all:

When I return to my same daily routine
that fed the landscape
which allowed your husband and eight others
to be assassinated during a June-time prayer circle

When today at dismantling racism
workshops
I make it all about me
speaking and sobbing uncontrollably
when I can no longer escape
these truths

When I talk about
purple people and say I'm colorblind
or treat you like you're nothing more
than a reaction to my whiteness

In all these ways and more
black woman
I
white woman
have betrayed you.

So now
standing on this earth
where God has delivered us both
I take the first step to be here
honest
asking and expecting nothing from you

(I have taken or tried to take so much)

Instead:
listening
when you speak, without interrupting;
not lying and cheating and stealing from
you and your family;
moving out your God-driven way instead of
making so many obstacles.

I will stop raising sons
who pull triggers instead of asking questions

I will not marry or silently indulge men
whose livelihoods are rooted in self-serving lies and
exploitation

I will say to politicians & police officers:
"Be in service of people
not racism
or your time in that job will be up."

From me, daughters will hear
These stories you're being told by
newscasters, movies, songs
saying "black is" one thing or another,
none of it whole-human, beautiful
pictures of "angry black women", "bad black parents", "hoes", "wel-
fare queens" —
They are not true;
do not repeat them.
Interrupt them.

When friends come
desperate to validate themselves by
helping "poor black people"
as school teachers or non-profit workers

Hand in Hand

I will help them see
what was shown to me
how "charity"
is needed only because old wide
systems of lovelessness, theft and violence are still with us.

Your soul is weak now, I will say to them, *together let's grow it strong.*

Then we—all of us delivered to this earth now—
can walk in ways
black
woman
that
do not betray you.

Kenneth Denk

Heritage

In a city that was never white
whether measured by population
or the integration of blood
and sweat of slaves laid into the
wood and stone of finely wrought
Antebellum opulence,
when a proudly flown banner is a
constant, subdermal sneer, muttering,
"Know Your Place, Boy,"
then your heritage is hate.
When the sacred silk on your flagpole
is no different, but for paint and patterns,
than the soot—stained sheets worn
by terrorists and cowards in the night,
too brave to do the hard work
of thinking and growing,
when that divergent pigment
in the skin is sin in your lily-white,
Southern Plight sight,
then your heritage is hate.
When black mothers weep and wail,
children, husbands, families ripped away
centuries ago or today,
but you care more for who marries whom
than innocent people filling tombs,
since they were probably thugs,
involved in drugs,
or sat their waiting to die,
your argument a twangy, ignorant lie
and your heritage is hate.

Miss me, with that
weak-sauce whitesplaining,
don't piss on my leg
and tell me it's raining,
your vaunted heritage
never stood for me
and if you were smart,
you wouldn't stand for it,
step clear of the shadow of the past
reaching long fingers
from beyond the grave,
last shovelful tossed and tamped
at a table in Appomatox,
don't dig to unearth old treason,
there a reason it's dead,
let it rest.

Roll the Stone

As the embers cool,
what's left of walls that
once filled with hallelujahs
tick and settle and sigh
with the dissipation
of heat, of hate,
that blazed from acts
too cowardly for the
light of day.
The irony that these arsonists
would clothe themselves
in the glorious mantle
of good Christians,
while burning a church,
is strong enough
for contact tetanus,
moving through the ruins.

Men with mean little souls
motivated by fear
know so little of the faith
they profess, or they'd know
that Christianity is about
Resurrection,
a temple torn down
will be rebuilt;
buildings burn easy,
but faith is fireproof,
and death has no dominion
in this place.

Worthy Evans

What We Do with the News from Africa

Upon hearing of unrest
in Uganda
and pictures and footage
of violence
during elections in the capital
of Kampala
I get reminded of Kamala,
the 6-feet-7inch, 380-pounder
who was a youngster,
a professional wrestler without a hook
until Jerry Lawler and some other people
painted stars on his chest
a crescent moon on his broad stomach
and a wild skeletal pattern on his face
and called him Kamala,
the Ugandan Giant,
because in the 1970s there happened to be
election unrest and death in Uganda
that made the television in Tennessee
and inspired a fearsome opponent
for ordinary wrestlers rolling around
in conventional red underpants.
This Kamala the Ugandan Giant
lumbered into the ring
with bare feet and a leopard print skirt.
He slapped his moon belly
and trampled littler boys
until they rolled on their backs as planned

until somebody pinned him.
Hooks can boost careers
but eventually wrestling moves on to bigger fears
such as communism and motorcycle gangs.
And the feeling that everything you work for
is never enough.
Kamala went on to ring after ring for thirty years
until as James Harris he lost one leg to diabetes
and then another. He is long retired
and still living in his hometown
of Senatobia, Mississippi.

Nancy Fierstein

A Wooden Cross Can Bear the Flames

for First Baptist Church, Dripping Springs, TX

Empty pews, one piano,
sheet music and psalms,
roof rafters and roofing –
each wafted, along

with black smoke, to the blue
skies which hovered above.
Come, sift through the ashes now.
Learn about love.

See the church which belongs now
to heavens once lit
with the flames that consumed
nearly each bit of it –

all but its wood cross,
which by heat was not doomed!
Love's message stands still,
just as when it first bloomed.

Keith Flynn

Look For Me In Liberia

for Nina Simone

What may come
when I sing
Sometimes my voice
is gravel
sometimes
coffee and cream
I splintered
ingested and embraced
Bach
I change keys
right in the middle
Where do I belong?
Wherever the edge is
free from fear

All power is black
the ebony squirrels
on the terrace
we ain't made friends
with them yet
Velvet wallpaper
makes the bathroom
feel more blue
Diamonds pasted
on my eyelids
and eyebrows
the balcony of my face

The fugue
and counterpoint
makes a high priestess
soul sound
sophisticated
and if they
can't learn to listen
I'll quit
Fuck it
Some dumbass bitch
in the audience
sweating me
I've swallowed the storm
I'll not be rode
I'm a freight train
I tell the track
where to go

He beat me
all the way home
Nobody seen me
for two weeks
All the way
in the elevator
up the stairs
He beat me
wham
into a concrete wall
He tells me
I want to be hit
I need it
the scars
he says
to stay straight

Everybody knows
about Mississippi
children's brains
scattered
in the sanctuary
Birmingham
and the Bull
got me so upset
bombs in my brain
Selma in my nightgown
goddam
Daddy says
I'm sidetracked
strange fruit
hanging from
the Southern trees
fire hoses opened up
Backlash
is the leather
on this breeze
says Stokely
squeezing
me

I'm bathing
in Bloody Marys
addled
and I leave em
with the blues
NC backwoods
or cold ass
Carnegie Hall
UNITED SNAKES
OF AMERICA
I want to shake
people free

of their elegant
smugness
and drive
their shriveled hips
insane

18,000 students
at the University
of Massachusetts
300 painted black
I quit singing
for anybody else
I want to see
them burn
curious
about themselves
I want to sing
a dagger
into the sick center
of the American soul
I want to cut
the twisted tail
from the world's
largest hog
They don't know
that I'm
already a ghost
wailing descended
backbone
howls

Matthew Foley

Soldiers of Love

after the 1963 March on Washington

Come back, you soldiers of love.
Come back, you strong of spirit and spine, unbroken.

Come back, you torchbearers of Gandhi's flame.
Come back, you who walked to freedom barefoot and bold.

Come back, you beaters of swords into plowshares.
Come back, you who went to the riverside and studied war no
more.

Come back, we need you now.

Come back, you who shook the sleeping from their dreamless
sleep.
Come back, children of Birmingham and children of Selma.

Come back, singers of songs to shake these prison walls.
Come back, poets of streets and sweet valleys we've never
known.

Come back, you whom tanks and bullets will not turn away.
Come back, you players of this symphony of brotherhood.

Come back, let us hear your song again.

Come back, Dr. King, come back.
Make us believe that you never truly left.

That every time we lift what has been beaten down,
you are there.

That every time we love what we have been told not to love,
you are there.

That every time we know that peace is the way,
you are there.

Be with us now, you soldiers of love.
Be with us now, Dr. King.
Be with us now.

Nikky Gray

Outside My Window

How is it there is laughter outside my window
That I hear banter outside my window
Life carrying on outside my window
As if they too weren't trapped in this causality loop of hatred,
racism, and death
As if their skin, like mine, kissed by the sun
wasn't also a bulls-eye
a black dot in a white world
waiting to be fired upon, choked out
broken, beaten, killed

How is it the streets are silent
That the wails of anguished mothers, fathers,
brothers, sisters, sons and daughters
do not pierce the air, drowning us in their sorrows
Too many forced to nurse their pain voiceless
How is it that black blood is so easily white-washed away
As if it was never spilled
As if it didn't matter

How is it that today looks like yesterday
That progress looks like an illusion we foolishly believed in
and the changes made only temporary Band-aids to a wound
in need of surgery
How is it that the sacrifice of our ancestors has been
forgotten
Their struggle forgotten
Their hardship forgotten
The lessons learned forgotten

How is it today looks like yesterday
That we've gone backwards
instead of moving forward

How is it the storm hasn't been noticed
the dark clouds rolling in
Thunder gathering strength
its force anger boiling over
Lightning striking all in its path
How is it the alarms haven't sounded
that the signs haven't been noted
that the danger is being ignored
Until... it is too late

Yuriy Grigoryants
Ain't That Crazy?

I was called son, father
Dumb Russian, Angry Armenian,
Brother,
Pretender, Comedian, Philosopher, Lover,
Stupid, intelligent,
Dear husband,
Freakin' immigrant,
Big Kahuna,
Good man,
A crazy mixture.

Also,
Deep, shallow...
I can't even swallow
All of this!
Sir, ma'am, shrink, dear doctor,
Do I have a
Multiple personalities disease?!
Hell, no!
I am an immortal soul
I am a part of the creation.
You were made with the same intention
Not to mention
That all definitions of oneself are false,
Except that
We are immortal souls.
A family with the same Daddy,
Yet afraid of each other...
Ain't that crazy?

Let me say it again my brother
Let me say it again my sister...
No, we are not asleep,
We're just blinking
Very slowly,
And I'm going to say it again
(Out of love, solely)

I am an immortal soul
I am a part of the creation
You were made with the same intention
Not to mention
That all definitions of oneself are false,
Except that
We are immortal souls
A family with the same Daddy,
Yet afraid of each other...
Ain't that crazy?

Ashley Harris

Savages

Savages, Savages, Barely even human!
Drag them from our shore, they're not like you and me,
Which means they must be evil
We must sound the drums of waaaar!

Those words my roommate spoke can never be drawn back,
The shots rung throughout my body,
They flowed down the tongue of her ignorance as she spat
Saliva Bible passages to salivate my indigenous instincts
So my identity would be easier for her to stomach

You eat like a Savage; I helped you become more acceptable
to society
Each harsh consonant you spoke sounded like correctional
facilities
Metal ropes African Americans are thrown through and or-
ange jumpsuits that put them
In their place like the bands of dollars jails count
Underneath the terrain of your white privilege my roots are
splitting pavements
And pumping drums of war to my heart louder
Than your police sirens

You think your money can control me like slavery
That your dollar signs can chain me to your colonies
Don't you feel so amazing? I bet helping me feels a lot like
Saving children in Haiti
Or finally paying attention to the aftermath of Kony
I am not your charity; you will not auction me away from my
mother
by telling me you would have done a better job at raising me,

In this world...
Where swollen pus wounds of whips aren't enough to distin-
guish my heritage
The rotting of strong opaque flesh in your negligence
Isn't a good enough explanation to why Martin Luther King
has a holiday
How many young men will have to be gunned down for you
to realize
I'm making a difference?

If a black man is hung at 90 degrees
How many swings will it take for you to see my history?
This is not The Blindside. That is the majority.
There are specs from your color spectrum that actually spot
me
I paint graffiti from the water color of my tears
On your blank canvas to show you
I was never chipping

The Bronx is still burning
In Virginia, Nat Turner is still living, in me
& your abolition abolishes my identity
I feel like an offering being passed around by your bidding
How many people in my family do you have to buy until you
own me?

I feel the squeezing of nooses around my neck
While you try to fit me into a suit more your size
As if my people haven't had to bleed enough so I could sit
among you bullet proof
Fredrick Douglass said it best
One and God make a majority
Every day I am accused of a false crime underneath your jury

No one is free until ethnicity is underneath the nation's feet
& individuality is crushed in the hands of Lady Liberty

Some slaves loved to be slaves because their masters were so
nice to them
You think you know me because you took African American
studies?
Your halo of light burns me like those old crosses in DC...

You can't control me. Doesn't my American name already
baptize me
Into the red, white, and blue you branded into my ancestors
flesh
Savages, Savages, barely even human...
Funny, in this world, people still
Don't get it

Simon Says

Me and my cousin used to play Simon Says

Simon says, Jump up and down!
Simon says, Laugh real loud!

We just go by what the grown folk say now

Auntie says to me, "Where are your breasts, I can't find them,"
says, "Ever consider surgery? Next Christmas I will get you extra padding."

Simon says, Find your chest!

Momma says, "How much is boob surgery again?"

Simon says, Find your chest!

Granny says, "Ain't you embarrassed yo' cousin wear a bigger bra size than you?
This is how I got yo' granddaddy."

Simon says, Find your chest!

Granny says my cousin is a tomato. I'm a stick.
The men don't fetch less the bait is thick.

Simon says, Find your chest!

Granny says to my cousin, "Mmm, mmm, fat, fat in all the wrong places…"

Simon says, Suck it in!

Granny says to me, "Don't let ya' cousin sit on legs, she might break 'em…"

Simon says, Suck it in!

Momma says to me, "When I was yo' age, I would just stuff 'em wit wash rages …"

Simon says, Stuff it in!

Momma says. "Poor folk these days can't afford pretty…"

Simon says, Be pitied!

Momma says to me, " …Least you got hips…"

The girls down the street say they want legs thin as the women in Vogue.

Simon says, Pose!

But I say my body is a funhouse mirror: bottom blown up, top shrunk.

Simon says, Pose!

Granny says. "…Least she ain't as dark as me…That's one good thing…"

Simon says, Run from the sun!

Auntie says, "ambi keeps you fair, your cousin needs some"

Simon says, Run from the sun!

Momma says, "Yo' cousin black as a boot!"

Simon says, Run from the sun!

The boys say, "I'd still mess wit' you two…"

Hand in Hand

Simon says, Smile

Me and my cousin say that makes us happy

Simon says, Smile

I say, "Well, why does that make us happy?"

Simon didn't say speak out! You're out!

We've become all fake, all face, all hate

My cousin says to me, "Hey ugly! Look at yo' flat chest!"

I say, "Look at you, blackie!"

We say silence…

Simon says, Wallow in the pain

Our lives are a game of head nods and OK's

Simon says, Swallow the pain

It's as if we're still playing

Simon says, Eat every word I say

Simon says…

Rashida James-Saadiya

Sweet Home

In Louisiana on February 1, 1996, a group of churches within six miles, Cypress Grove Baptist, St. Paul's Free Baptist, Thomas Chapel Benevolent Society in East Baton Rouge, and Sweet Home Baptist in Baker were each set on fire on the 36th anniversary of the Greensboro, North Carolina sit-in.

What I remember
ember resting on hands
blood
hidden in the pleats of my dress

bones scattered beneath our feet
prayers hanging off lips
curved over
like innocence
pushed against the hurt

bodies bent and rocking,
a hymn
full of broken pieces
with no place to go

the spirits
we walk on
won't lay down
they want glory
or something to wash
the stench away

How does it feel ?
to be alive and unwanted
like an eruption of skin
a knife born into your heart
a thousand screams
clutching the sky

the words are caught in my throat
all we have is burning
red, blazing and bright
a sign the living can read
heat that will melt your mouth
crawl up your spine
remind you of
night riders,
gripping kerosene

enough matches
to take your breath away
this story is made of bones
aching for tomorrow
what waits behind the trees
across the old tracks

history coming to set your day on fire

Honoree Fanonne Jeffers

Singing Counter

after Hayes and Mary Turner, Valdosta, Georgia, May 1918

The rope, the tree,

the tired comparison to Jesus on the Cross. Avoid the tropes.

The metaphors.
This stands for that, but if no one black ever says that, how
would

someone white learn
this? How would any of us? I desire the surprise of
intellectual,

fractured lyrics.
Yet here I am, refusing refusal. Calling the mob out by name.

Not even safely—
as with an anonymous South—but uncomfortably. As with
white

man by white man.
(I'm scared just saying it.) And locating each in case

you have trouble.
(My People are exceedingly patient.) There: the expected

poor, drunk one,
neck darkened in the field. He's a nice cliché. But not the
next:

a churchgoer
and father. A man who believes in Christ and the love of a
virtuous

woman who fries
chicken for picnics and stirs up lemon cakes. After the
lynching

he will continue
to believe and live his life in a good fashion. Beside him, his
little boy,

smiling, his teeth
only beginning to loosen as he moves from baby to heir. He
will grow,

remember his father's
beauty, the godly meat in that chest. In the back of this
crowd,

a young scholar
home from college, brought by his friends who wanted to see

if what their science
professor said was true, that niggers did not feel pain the
same

as better men.
Too old for the rowdy festival, someone's grandfather

remains at home.
An educated-in-the-North patrician who owns the newspaper

that later will run
the story. A savage raised his voice to a man. (One tenor

singing counter
to the other.) Or, he asked for his pay on Friday. Or, he

did not dance
when desired. Or, he did not step off the sidewalk for a lady.

(Should I explain
the Southern Anthropological Equation of lady plus race?)

Her flowered honor
required protecting. The imperative of her womanhood:

ax and gasoline
and black blood. Pig-like screams of what is not a man to the mob,

but a side
of meat. What never was in this place. I will admit these things

in my contemporary
time, but not out loud. My white friends and colleagues

(who are not
My People) would feel indicted by my saying, I look at you
and yes,

I'm frightened.
I wonder if you would have sliced off my toe as I hung there,
roasting over

the slowest fire
the mob could build. And later, killed my pregnant wife, the baby

still inside her.
I'm a sinner. I fear what I crave. Or love. Part of the falling,

the romance,
is a quandary keeping the present here. The past there.

Hand in Hand

A liquid-filled jar
of sex in a general store: before that day, its name was Hayes.

He made the mistake
of calling to her. Mary answered, her hand resting on her
belly.

Draft of an Ex-Colored Letter Sent Home From the Post-Race War Front

A soldier in Baldwin's Country & I can't even dance
I say you can't beat me   Each day I get up to face fear
again

I made money & fixed my credit   I escaped you dear   my
shame
Yet how to escape white space   It's impossible

to return to your embrace to rough-trading sweet vowels
to brothers on corners visiting my dreams   I hear your
whistles

Smell Mama's collard greens on suburban wind   I love you
with deception
I'll be back   I'll lift as I climb   My remorse goes deep

to the whiteness in me   my bones   Forgive me   You
don't know
the trouble I see   I can't tell these folks the truth

They don't understand me & they don't try   Or they try too
hard
I want my birthright   a mutual sight   my own ancient
rime

In the bright trenches of the office   I open my mouth but
choke
on bottled water   Last week   I returned for your wake

& left before the home-going   I miss our surviving dark
ones

67

Hand in Hand

The familiar is trivial & profound   The strange a charge

in my blood   I clutch & shriek at these strangers I left
drums for
I sing B.B.'s mean old song

Ashley M. Jones

Water

for Flint, MI

I am three, and suddenly a nagging thirst
consumes me. There is only the want,
the aching, quick-heeled pull of water,
the sink filled with a stagnant, cloudy pool
and my Dixie cup, dipping—
I never really tasted the bleach, its poison

turning the water a salty white, poison
which, in washwater, sucks out stains with a chemical thirst,
and here, my mother had opened the bottle's plastic mouth,
drizzled
the bleach in standing water to clean the porcelain bowl—she
wanted,
as always, a house above the greasy pull
of germs, but all she did was taint the water,

left it waiting for me, girl wanting water,
to blindly drink without permission or reason. But at least
that poison
was bottled and labeled. In Flint, the water is a pool
of invisible danger, slick. Still water enough to quench the
thirst
of all those drinking citizens—what more could they want?
What you don't know can't hurt, but what you don't drink?

Even lead can be liquid, can drip
into a silent blade. How is it that even bathwater
can kill—the bubbles and their phosphorescent shine want
to wrap you in their glistening, clear-sphered poison,

drink you down to the last drop, thirsty
as a child. What is power that it can pool

and rush through pipes, it can waterfall, whirlpool,
seep its way even into our homes, into the dripping
kitchen faucet, into our open cups, turning our thirst
to suicide, our lives at the mercy of water.
Even when I drank the bleach, when I sipped the poison
at three years old, it was just a little dirty water—

I could recover from its tiny poison, its one-time pool
of murky chemical want. All of you who thirst
in Flint: when will water be water again, not a death-knell, a
fatal drip?

Fayaz Kabani

Dominant Genes

I wonder if, in a couple generations
when the AppleFaceGoo administration's
running the country, or maybe just the world,
after I have fostered children with a white girl
and they've fallen in love and settled down and sown
their seed (and so on), will those kids know their fountain-
head was brown,
Ismaili Muslim, the son of decently well-off Ugandan refu-
gees
who left their lives and servants to work in car and textile
factories,
that I got racially slurred, called "Haji" (my dad's dad's name),
when I wore my winter beard,
or will they think, "My great-granddad was Indian. Now ain't
that weird?"

Len Lawson

America.

A dark-skinned mother of triplets weeps
holding the infants for the first time.

With sweat pooling in her gullet
she announces to the hospital room

These children will be called
Ferguson, Baltimore, and Charleston.

The babies cycle around
the room through many hands.

A nurse conveys the news of
their names to the father in

the waiting area. He glances
at the rapid fire sun rioting

through the window.
Sweat angers a necklace

around his beige button shirt.
A terror slaps his eyes

back at her like daggers.
He cuts her in a whisper

I have babies being born
to weeping mothers

all over this country

Right now!

Tell me their names!
Tell me they matter!

Black Boy Talking Rivers

after Langston Hughes

I ain't talking   no chilly Jordan
                no down by the riverside
                no crossing to that other shore

I'm talking place that looks like where the slave ship dropped us off

I'm talking place where we washed the blood from the whips and fists out our clothes

I'm talking place in the Mother Land where we get dragged away by crocodiles, hippos, and anacondas while fetching water

I'm talking place where we get tied dead to a fan slicing our faces up for surrendering to the crystal waters in a white woman's eyes

and they wonder why we don't swim

Bleach

n. 1) A chemical agent that removes color or whitens

v. 2) To become whiter or lighter in color

A chemical solvent but what can it solve
Blots out transgressions but not like God
I still see what he forgets and ignores. It solved his son
Before the white shores of Plymouth Rock landed on him

Inhale this solution and it strips away membranes
Rumbles the tectonic plates of my mind
If I baptize myself in it enough times
My soul becomes gentrified

The sound of its name sends chills through my blackness
Pour some on the word nigger and watch a black man dance
and sing for millions
Pour some on the black man and watch him be sold to the
highest bidder
While he still dances to the jangle of his neck shackle

A household remedy to silence the bite of the black house-
hold
Teach me the chemical equation for blackness
Gather me the elements to the formula for reparations &
Justice for every black woman slave raped &

Every black family broken up in the name of white econom-
ics &
For removing the scars (no not figurative scars, literal scars)
Carving out crop circles and line segments on wasted black
backs
Or ask Rachel Dolezal how to mix her potion for blackness
with

Spray tan, weave, and occasional black ignorance when it
seems funny
Even to black people but the word jigaboo doesn't look
appropriate
For appropriation on 99¢ jugs with white and black sale signs
over them
Can't tell me this stuff cleans and disinfects leaving behind
the smell of genocide

Bring forth the black alchemist, not the mad scientist that
yielded Elvis Pressley, Eminem,
Gwen Stefani, Fergie, Macklemore, Iggy Azalea, and every kid
in the suburbs
Whispering white power in their closets at home afraid in
their high schools of the black cliques
Their forefathers cornered the market on fear long before the
word thug was a tissue to wipe up

Black culture from the corners of white lying mouths
Bullets are the bleach their sons use to cleanse the earth from
black bodies
But the odor from their ethnic cleansing rises to white heaven
where
A little boy with a racist daddy dies and claims to have seen
black jesus

White lies seem not to make it past the white light when they
black out
The chemical crystal waters have covered the earth like a
Sherwin Williams paint can
For millennia resulting in a chemical reaction called race
Bleach is not water; it wants to be water. It is only
appropriating water.

Reparations

after Ta-nehisi Coates

Great-granddaddy's acres
now a white man's oil field
Grass Great-great-grandmama
could have rippled her

tired dusty toes through freely
now center field for a minor league
baseball park. Great-great-great uncle's
favorite horse robbed from him blind

for a concussion and forced to mate
century after century with other robbed
horses to breed Secretariat &
American Pharaoh & Big Brown &

You Don't Whistle At No White Woman
& Skittles and Tea & Arms Like the Hulk &
Can't Breathe & Eight Shots To The Back
With a Taser By His Side & We Grew Millions

From Rows Of Welts On Slave Backs
Great-granddaddy's country club now
the vapor of an echo in a dream from his grave
Great-great-grandmama's sweet cane fields

now the rejected prayer to
sweet milky white baby jesus
Great-great-great Uncle's filly still
making sweet love to that blue donkey

sniffing for votes every four years
but that love child mule dead
in a forty-acre wasteland like
hope, like change, like dismembered

disemboweled nigger dreams

When Santa Claus Visits the Home of Tamir Rice

'Twas the night Casper of Cleveland Christmases Past
      hovered at his tree unseen by his mother at the fire
An opulent white man's boots soggy from the river of tears
      leading to her inflamed weary eyes

Peering down the chimney, the old man stared down the
barrel of her screams
      Not another white man will come for my boy's body
Sound of sleigh bells swallowed by gun shots
      on a continual loop in the mother's mind

Crush red velvet jacket lamenting black blood
      on the boy's shirt from his crushed black body
Trample of reindeer hooves stifled by the march of
      police boots treading the boy's dreams under foot

He may have dreamed of being a policeman
      He may have been shooting bad guys the moment
he was thrust from fantasy into the black reality of the
afterlife
      The jolly ol' elf's Ho, ho, ho thundering down the
black

hole transmogrified into the mother's heaving, screeching
      moaning, courthouse column-crumbling throat
Justice may be blind but the mother determines it can't be
deaf
      It must hear / Its ears must bleed / It must be
exposed to its own

crush red velvet within its body the way her baby was ex-
posed to his
      Why should justice prevent her baby from breathing

79

while a white stranger, a bearded white god saddled with
presents dwelling
    above reproach atop the globe, is encouraged to bur-
den her roof

with no police guns drawn / The boy awaited the best gift
ever
    with toy gun in hand / for his life back

The woman prayed to the true Giver of Gifts
    for the old white man to be unarmed

Scott Murray

Cousin-hood...

On empty page or canvas
myriads of methods,
words approach
sonnets emerge
driven shapes
not from nowhere
finished article
accounted for by completion...

Movement from Africa
webbed trails
knotted together
de-constructed D.N.A
trails us all
back home
we stand universally
completion of cousin-hood...

Kathleen Nalley

Pangaea

Before us, before concrete structures and paved roads,
        before people cultivated and grew, 225 million years
ago,
                the continents were joined, Africa and
the Americas
                        were one land:

        today's Charleston cupped today's Sahara.
When plates shifted, when land moved farther
                        away from land, the Atlantic
became
        an ocean between.

If you look at the continents on a globe,
you can see how their boundaries
        connected, once,
                how South Carolina's coastline hugged
Africa's
        northwestern curve, how Africa's northwestern curve
hugged
South Carolina's coastline,

back then, 225 million years ago, before us, when all was
whole.

Jerlean Noble

Bring It Down

Bring it down
The chants were led
By those who were shouting
For those who are dead

I shouted loud
With the massive crowd
Covering statehouse grounds
It's time to come down

I cried tears
For my family and me
Who fought for years
To be recognized free

It took the death of nine
Courageous souls
For that Confederate flag
To come down with its pole

Donald Pardlow

A Typical Faculty-lounge Debate

"They took genetic samples from the grave
of Thomas Jefferson and found he had
several children by his own slaves . . . .
Why in the world did they have to do that?
If old Tom were alive to hear,
he would roll over in his grave!"
The only male among the group, I said
nothing, yet I was not the only black . . . .

"Oh, yeah! He would roll over, to Sally,
or a wench on the opposite side!
He played God with a thousand black women!
He thought nothing of it, and if he did,
he'd leap out of his grave and just click his heels!

And yell, 'Oh, yeah! Now those was the days!'"

Pasckie Pascua

Nomads

We are nomads.
We are bastard children of volcanic wrath
cactus thorns cut up from their mothers' limb
by fugitive Siberian winds
and pulled toward Pacific Coast Highway
by Queen Isabella's buffalo soldiers.

Our grandmothers are Cherokee nightingales
lost along Trail of Tears on Interstate 40
on their way to Foxworth Casino,
our grandfathers are Malayan cave dwellers
of Astronesian blood
adapted by Spanish conquistadores
and exhibited at the St Louis World's Fair.

Our sisters have kingfisher eyes
snagged by prodigal pirates
off South China Sea
and then sold to Uncle Sam's
foreign policy's R&R,
our brothers bear pagan machetes
slayer of intruders
with crucifixes on their foreheads—
blood dripping down
their mortgaged faces.

We are nomads.
Spare change thrown
onto a grimy fountain of doom

after the Treaty of Paris
sealed our fate following

the defeat of the Spanish Armada
by the Desert Storms
of our AmEx lives
and Wells Fargo valentines,
like scripted coup d'etats
played out of Hollywood brothels
on gilded screens as huge as
undernourished Third World chests.

We are the scar of the 4th streets
of the Main Streets of American heartland--
the rolling stones of downtown Manhattans
down West 4ths toward Bleecker streets
uptown Capitol Hills at the curb
of Dow Jones Boulevards
of the U S of A's of our credit card dreams,
the remnants of 700 bottles of bourbon
seeking warmth by the dumpsters
of decay and doom
from Chicago to Las Vegas,
Newark, New Jersey to Flint, Michigan
from the slums of our winter delusions
to the JFK Airports of
our neverending journeys.

We are nomads.
We feed on faces and places
nameless sidestreets, forgotten alleyways
we dine on words strewn by the gutters
cold and hard but alive.
We are nomads, I am a nomad—
a seeker of truths in American sidestreets
and a poet with one million immigrant
wounds.

Michele Reese

Six Stars Market

Two cans stand on the curb
under cumulus clouds.

One man with his hood
down paces, watching

the tree-lined street.
Others wait with him.

The SUV pulls
onto the sidewalk.

Two doors open,
guns train, pop,

stretch yellow tape
and excuses.

Jonathan K. Rice

Falling Down

Young black man runs
from security guards,
cop wanna-be's
who think he's up to no good.

They know he's going to steal,
probably already did
but he's not carrying anything
that they can see.

He's just running.

They chase him in a vehicle,
cutting him off across the street,
almost hitting him
near an exit ramp.

It's dark. He's out of breath.
They yell, put up your hands!
He raises his arms,
but only has one hand.

I didn't do nothin'!

One guard cuffs him,
but a handcuff slips off
with no hand
to hold it in place.

They all wait for the police.
When officers arrive

the young man's head is bleeding,
his mouth and one eye are swollen.

One guard explains, he fell down.

King Shakur

21 Reasons He Ran

for Walter Scott

1.   For the same reason she clutches her purse as he gets on the elevator

2.   For the same reason you cross to the other side of the street when you see a group of him together

3.   Because he could still hear Tamir Rice's cries, and Eric Garner's choking voice saying he can't breathe

4.   Because whether he has a GED, BA, MBA or PHD, he will always fit the description

5.   Because there is a perpetual APB out for a black male between the ages of 12-72 standing between 4"5 and 7ft tall, weighing between 80 and 350 pounds

6.   Because men with wooly hair and bronze skin have a loooong history of being persecuted

7.   Because he hadn't learn to bend the spoon or dodge bullets

8.   Because the kiwi is not the strange fruit Nina was singing about

9.   Because Charles S. Dutton told us in Menace II Society "Being a Black Man in America isn't easy...The hunt is on and we're the prey!"

10.   Because for some reason in a Black man's hand, a wallet looks a lot like a gun

11.   Because he was trying to catch that elusive 2/5th of himself that was taken away in the early 1600's

12.   He felt the spirits of Kunta, Denmark, Harriett, Nat

13.   And Fred, Amadou, Trevon, Oscar, and Sabrina

14.   Because justice may be blind but she has a nose for melanin

15.   Because racists didn't get the memo that America is now post-racial

16.   Because he read the 13th Amendment

17.   Because of Reaganomics, the Three Strikes laws, NAFTA, NDAA

18.   Because there were no Black folks on the Jetsons (he was not supposed to be a part of the future)

19.   He didn't have George and Weezy's luck

20.   And Barney Fife never minded taking a life

21.   1619, 1776, 1863, Juneteenth....AmeriKKKa!!!

Charlene Spearen

We Are the Nine ...

...like the pause/between dusk and darkness
between fury and peace,
but, for such as our earth is now...
Derek Walcott

i

Rev. Depayne Middleton Doctor
Baby, pin a star on me.
Come quickly, see the light in my eyes,
call me lady. This lady blossomed
four dazzling girls, and like fallen leaves,
a natural reshaping of what was
into what is good. I embrace God's way
of being the helping hand that moves winter
into spring, growing back flowers: black-eyed susans,
imnpatiens, golden marigolds that smile back
at the sun. I will, with the Lord's helping hand,
grow the flower of forgiveness while I continue
to live-out inside the light of your imagination.

ii

Cynthia Hurd
Baby, pin a star on me.
The lord's word was written down
in a great book, and I heard His message,
heard right from the start the music of words,
the rhythm of serving the notes of learning,
Knowledge unlocking-click
Minds unlocking-click

Growing in the light-click
Understanding the lost energy of a frown-click

Respect for what the lord gives-click-click
How a misshapen view, like a pulled trigger-bang-bang,
can teach us how to live inside the fire of absolution.

iii
Susie Jackson
Baby, pin a star on me
The winds of time cycled a good many paths
through my garden, and honey there is no use
bringing politics into my journey, we all know
Jim Crow, his story. Crows still eat the budding corn,
rioting words still, like spilled honey, spread over
a baby's cinnamon skin.
I am now still and cold
so sing to me of hanging stars
church hymns that rock the altar
and dark trees that can never hide the rising sun.

iv
Ethel Lance
Baby, pin a star on me.
I know the meaning of real work
how to serve the lord, the shaft of pain,
how sitting idle can invite the devil in
can come dressed in an innocent face
sheep's clothing (black churches never
were a safe place), but share this, on Sunday morning
I was Ms. Ethel: the whistle in my step, reading the bible,
worship, church folk gathering! Amen!
God's house was always my palace. Honey, never
get lost in the motion, despair's bottomless sea, never
bury hope in the past, stare-down hypocrisy
conjure out of this ruthless act the rising of a new day.

93

v

The Rev. and SC State Senator Clementa Pinkney
Baby, pin a star on me.
I know many houses swim with tortured
elocution, ugly words roll off tongues
like a fired gun. This is why God told me
to walk with all my brothers and sisters,
to preach his word, we are their keepers.
Friends, go down the road
go, then, go to where action affirms God-given rights
move, roll magic, a holy drum roll, be like a preacher
preaching the miracle of mercy.
Wash this church clean, go forth, go forth
wash the world clean.

vi

Tywanza Sanders
Baby, pin a star on me.
Mom says I am her hero.
I never set out to be one, just wanted
to live, be a good Christian, be a good son
a good person, a good poet. To spread
a real message, make things better. O say can you
see...a better future, politicians always need new
jumpstarts, often willy-nilly waddle through fields
filled with white lilies. Snip, snip, buzz
buzz carry my name, all the blood flowing like
stoplights. There is always the need for hoodooing
new songs, new lyrics wooing daybreak while the cock
crowing three times. Celebrate the call and response
woven inside my shimmering poems and my words:
Why are you doing this...

vii
Brother, Rev. Dr. Lee Simmons
Baby, pin a star on me.

Our Father, Heavenly Father, Lord Father,
you have heard me pray these words
when despair's dark moan and creak
fills the soul. But today we are standing
on the deck of new beginnings. I want
to be in this, be with my family, my church family,
pray with the enemy who brings darkness
into a holy, summer, night, cry out Jesus,
hallelujah. Tell them not to give in, not one bit,
believe in God, always, His will
will be done. Night always ends with a clear
register for a new day, the hope of a holy amen.

viii
Rev. Sharonda Coleman-Singleton
Baby, pin a star on me.
I was transformed by love,
became a visible burning
in my home, my church, served all
saw no difference, really, Mother,
Mother Church, Mother World, Mother
Nature. All cupped in the hands of God.
I can walk in on a soft breeze or fly like a fly-ball
even when I was setting the Sunday-dinner table.
Time will pass, at first a moment here and there like
a fleeting world (we will soon breathe regular breaths
unfeeling as it seems) but always depend
on the Lord's promises, and how hitting a home-run
can happen inside one simple prayer.

ix
Myra Thompson
Baby, pin a star on me.
"Everyone who drinks of this water will thirst again;
but whoever drinks of the water that I will give him
shall never thirst…" Samaritan women are everywhere,
inside a classroom, inside the corner store, inside a church
placing flowers on an altar. Slowly like a photo taking form,
they shape the world. Teach, preach far and wide,
love, compassion, knowledge that expands the mind. Look
into
my round, brown, eyes, pocketbook my gentle smile, minister
the sick, sick of body, sick of mind. Keep a white dress, white
leather pumps, white gloves, white hat in your closet,
let your skin shine and remember we are the Emanuel Nine.

Tammaka Staley

Some men are not women-lovers.

Some men are not women-lovers.
Only intrigued by having women lovers. Weaned from bosom
long ago. Still clung to far-fetched ideas that a black woman's
nature can quench thirsty desires for happiness.
Never learned nipples were not created for pleasure.
Not made for their mouths to crucify or resurrect erections in
homes absent of holiness.
Calling her goddess does not mean you recognize the God in
her.

Some men be educated by the foolish.
Think, the darker your complexion
the more likely he can turn you into wine.
Mammify your magic.
Say, Closed mouths don't get fed.
Say, Your teeth only for chewing, makes it easy to swallow.
To digest.
To make a meal out of something that doesn't belong in belly.
Say red lipstick is   prettier   when
        smeared
when more pressure is applied.
Still, consent is sexy too.

Cassie Premo Steele

How White Women Live in South Carolina

Sunlight rusted through the hinges of existence
in the early spring after seasons of rain
on the morning we came from dreams of drowning.

You and I are still alive in the state where nine
were shot down four days after our wedding.
As women, we love in the aftermath of massacre.

Rust red brick dirt showed through white washed walls
in the early morning after months of silence
on the spring day we woke to hear poetry.

You and I are not yet deaf in the room where words
rise and split their heads against the concrete and we claim
the blood coming down like holy wine with our tongues.

Amoja Sumler

Carolina Blood Magic

Here blood means something. Blood is the honored artifact,
the keepsake staining skin into dimpled freckled smile,
life buried deep, betrayer of misborn secrets. Shit
on the tips of tongues. The Frenchman dabbled in dappled
skin. Some of his kin bore his name (some could bear the
lash).
Seed was for sowing, for bent Brown backs. Spread salvation!
It's Jeffersonian kindness, task of good White men,
an owner's burden. The yearning teacher's ritual.
Each stroke: a lesson in comeuppance for uppity
farm hands -- too tender to pick. 'Whollop the Nigger!' blood
moistens soil. Determination makes Denmark Vesey's.
Here when they run, we course bucks with coonhounds,
our Klan leaves 'em lay -- spilling, ruined like Golgotha.

Cedric Tillman

Tread on Me

We had the funeral for my freedom last night.
The right to life was 19 years old.
Freedom pulled a trigger and killed my freedom
because freedom trumps my freedom, is more precious
than my freedom. My freedom died for your freedom,
didn't enlist but it died for this country, by this country.
Guns don't kill freedom, freedom kills freedom.

The other day, the city said I could watch my freedom bleed
out real cheap
Said they'd take my taxes, let me see my freedom bleed out
for cheap
but freedom sued the city,
said I didn't have that kind of freedom.
ISP Freedom said I could feel free to pay them $39.95 a
month
for the privilege of seeing freedom bleed out on my PC,
assured me I'd get my money's worth, that freedom would see
to it.
The city infringed on Freedom's freedom to bind me.
I think I have to get more freedom if I wanna be free.

Freedom don't look good on my freedom,
see how it lies there, gashed through the body armor.
My freedom was in tech school, just welding,
just HVAC.
My freedom had college ID but I wish it had a freedom per-
mit.

The only thing freer than a gun with a bullet in the chamber
is the freedom pointing it at freedom.
Freedom breathes easier after it's loaded an AR-15.

Free to be bad assed, free to stand its ground.
Feel dat? All the heat and air
around an idea?
Freedom breathes like this——wishes somebody would
try to stop it from breathing the way it breathes.
The constitution of a semi-automatic's freedom
makes it easy to hyperventilate.

Arthur Turfa

Brief Elegy for a Burned-out Church

decades for building
an hour for burning:
bare-ruined choirs
where generations sang
and prayed for strength
to endure continued indignity,
now offer silent testimony
to the hatred of arsonists
who worship the same God
but hear only what
they want to hear.

Marjory Wentworth

Holy City

Only love can conquer hate.
Reverend Clementa Pinckney

Let us gather and be
silent together like stones
glittering in sunlight

so bright it hurts our eyes
emptied of tears and searching
the sky for answers.

Let us be strangers
together as we gather
in circles wherever we meet,

to stand hand in hand and sing
hymns to the heavens and pray
for the fallen and speak their names:

Clementa, Cynthia, Tywanza,
Ethel, Sharonda, Daniel,
Myra, Susie and Depayne.

They are not alone. As bells
in the spires call across
the wounded Charleston sky,

we close our eyes and listen
to the same stillness ringing
in our hearts, holding onto

one another like brothers,
like sisters because we know
wherever there is love, there is God.

Music of Doves Ascending

Yellow crime tape tied to the rod iron fence
weaves through bouquets of flowers
and wreaths made of white ribbons,
like rivers of bright pain flowing through the hours.

Weaving through bouquets of flowers,
lines of strangers bearing offerings
like rivers of bright pain flowing through the hours.
One week later; the funeral bells ring;

lines of strangers still bring offerings.
Nine doves tossed toward the sun.
One week later; the funeral bells ring,
while churches in small towns are burning.

Nine doves tossed toward the sun.
Because there are no words to sing,
while churches in small towns are burning,
a blur of white wings, ascends like music

One River, One Boat

In memory of Walter Scott

I know there's something better down the road.
-- Elizabeth Alexander

Because our history is a knot
we try to unravel, while others
try to tighten it, we tire easily
and fray the cords that bind us.

The cord is a slow moving river,
spiraling across the land
in a succession of S's,
splintering near the sea.

Picture us all, crowded onto a boat
at the last bend in the river:
watch children stepping off the school bus,
parents late for work, grandparents

fishing for favorite memories,
teachers tapping their desks
with red pens, firemen suiting up
to save us, nurses making rounds,

baristas grinding coffee beans,
dockworkers unloading apartment size
containers of computers and toys
from factories across the sea.

Every morning a different veteran
stands   at the base of the bridge
holding a cardboard sign
with misspelled words and an empty cup.

In fields at daybreak, rows of migrant
farm workers standing on ladders, break open
iced peach blossoms; their breath rising
and resting above the frozen fields like clouds.

A jonboat drifts down the river.
Inside, a small boy lies on his back;
hand laced behind his head, he watches
stars fade from the sky and dreams.

Consider the prophet John, calling us
from the edge of the wilderness to name
the harm that has been done, to make it
plain, and enter the river and rise.

It is not about asking for forgiveness.
It is not about bowing our heads in shame;
because it all begins and ends here:
while workers unearth trenches

at Gadsden's Wharf, where 100,000
Africans were imprisoned within brick walls
awaiting auction, death, or worse.
Where the dead were thrown into the water,

and the river clogged with corpses
has kept centuries of silence.
It is time to gather at the edge of the sea,
and toss wreaths into this watery grave.

And it is time to praise the judge
who cleared George Stinney's name,
seventy years after the fact,
we honor him; we pray.

Hand in Hand

Here, where the Confederate flag flew
beside the Statehouse, haunted by our past,
conflicted about the future; at the heart
of it, we are at war with ourselves

huddled together on this boat
handed down to us – stuck
at the last bend of a wide river
splintering near the sea.

Contributors

Dasan Ahanu is an artist, educator, and organizer living in Durham, NC. In addition to performing, Dasan has hosted or coordinated many cultural arts events. He has been featured on national radio and TV, published three books of poetry, and released a number of hip hop and spoken word recordings.

Marcus Amaker is the first Poet Laureate of Charleston, SC. He's released seven books, a poetry app, and more than fifteen albums of original music. One of those albums *The New Foundation* was recorded with Grammy-nominated drummer and producer Quentin E. Baxter. Marcus was recently featured on PBS Newshour. In addition to poetry and music, Marcus is an award-winning graphic designer, web designer, and videographer. He is the former editor of the *Post and Courier*'s entertainment section, Charleston Scene.

Jennifer Bartell teaches at Spring Valley High School in Columbia, SC. She is a Callaloo Fellow and her work has been published in *Kakalak, The Raleigh Review, The Petigru Review, Callaloo Journal,* and *As/Us: Women of the World.*

Al Black was born and raised in Lafayette, IN. He is an administrator at the University of South Carolina. In 2014, he released his first poetry collection *I Only Left for Tea* (Muddy Ford Press). A *Jasper Magazine* Literary Artist of the Year nominee, he hosts several arts venues in Columbia, SC. He has been married 42 years to his wife Carol, and they have four children and nine grandchildren.

Bernard Block began his Poetry Series at Bowery Poetry Club. He hosted the next thirteen sequels at Cornelia Street Café, entitled "From Whitman to Ginsberg: Poems That Challenge Conventional Wisdom." All 14 editions are posted on YouTube. Twenty-three of his poems were published in the on-line European literary journal *Levure Litteraire* #8 and #9.

Kim Blum-Hyclak, a transplanted Buckeye, lives in Lancaster, SC. Her work has appeared in *Iodine Poetry Journal, Kakalak, Petigru Review,* and *Catfish Stew.* In 2015, her debut poetry collection *In the Garden of Life and Death* was published by Main Street Rag.

Roger Bonair-Agard, a native of Trinidad and Tobago, is a poet and performance artist who lives in Chicago. He has made numerous television and radio appearances, led countless workshops and lectures, and performed his poetry at many US universities as well as international festivals in Germany, Switzerland, Milan, and Jamaica. His most recent poetry collection *Bury My Clothes* was a 2013 National Book Award for Poetry finalist.

Fran Cardwell taught in the Columbia, SC Richland One School District for thirty years.

Cortney Lamar Charleston is a Cave Canem Fellow, Finalist for the 2015 Auburn Witness Poetry Prize, and Semi-finalist for the 2016 Discovery/Boston Review Poetry Prize. His poems have appeared or are forthcoming in *Beloit Poetry Journal, Gulf Coast, Hayden's Ferry Review, The Iowa Review, The Journal, New England Review, Pleiades, River Styx, Spillway, TriQuarterly* and elsewhere.

Tiana Clark is the author of the chapbook *Equilibrium,* selected by Afaa Michael Weaver for the 2016 Frost Place Chapbook Competition. She is the winner of the 2016 Academy of American Poets Prize and 2015 Rattle Poetry Prize. Tiana is an MFA candidate at Vanderbilt University where she serves as Poetry Editor for *Nashville Review.* She has received scholarships to The Sewanee Writers' Conference and The New Harmony Writers Workshop. Her writing has appeared or is forthcoming in *Best New Poets 2015, Crab Orchard Review, Southern Indiana Review, The Adroit Journal, Muzzle Magazine, Thrush Poetry Journal, The Offing,* and elsewhere.

Julia Dawson lives in Columbia, SC. In addition to poetry, she explores history with teenagers as a middle school teacher.

Kenneth Denk from Upstate New York is a father, nurse, and poet who now makes his home in Columbia, SC.

Worthy Evans is the author of *Green Revolver* (University of South Carolina Press, 2010). He is the 2015 winner of the Saluda River Prize for poetry presented by the Jasper Project. He is also a collage artist, with his work "House Hunters" appearing at the Columbia Museum of Art in 2015 as a part of the Columbia Broadside Project. When he is not cutting up images and rearranging them whether through poetry or collage, he is a Communications Specialist for a Medicare contractor in Columbia, SC.

Nancy Fierstein hosts Thirsty Thursday, a monthly venue open to poets, musicians, and storytellers, under her leadership since 2007. She is the editor of two Best Austin Poetry collections published by the Austin Poetry Society. A Pushcart Prize nominee, her work often appears in Texas Poetry Calendars and in anthologies by the Austin International Poetry Festival.

Keith Flynn is the award-winning author of seven books, including five collections of poetry: *The Talking Drum* (1991), *The Book of Monsters* (1994), *The Lost Sea* (2000), *The Golden Ratio* (Iris Press, 2007), *Colony Collapse Disorder* (Wings Press, 2013), and a collection of essays, entitled *The Rhythm Method, Razzmatazz and Memory: How To Make Your Poetry Swing* (Writer's Digest Books, 2007). His latest book is a collaboration with photographer Charter Weeks, entitled *Prosperity Gospel: Portraits of the Great Recession*. Flynn is founder and managing editor of *The Asheville Poetry Review*, which began publishing in 1994.

Matthew Foley is a writer, spoken word artist, and English teacher in Charleston, South Carolina. He has released two books of poetry *We Could Be Oceans* and *The Typewriter Sutra*, as well as a spoken word poetry album *What You Will Need in Class Today*. He currently teaches high school English as the Charleston County School of the Arts and is the founder of Holy City Youth Slam, an organization in Charleston that teaches poetry and performance to local youth.

Nikki Gray from Ann Arbor, MI, is a singer, songwriter, and poet currently residing in Atlanta, GA.

Yuriy Grigoryants emigrated from Russia to the US in 1998. He lived almost eleven years in New York and moved to San Antonio, TX, in 2009. He has published two books of poetry and short stories: *Burnt Lips* (2012) and *The Last Venus* (2015).

Ashley Harris is a poet and aspiring doctor who graduated from the University of North Carolina at Chapel Hill, majoring in chemistry and Hispanic culture and literature with a minor in creative writing. She was placed on the Brave New Voices youth slam team for Chapel Hill in 2011 and represented UNC-Chapel Hill in 2014 and 2015 at the College Unions Invitational Slam. Her work has been published in *Yellow Chair Review, Event Horizon,* and the bilingual magazine *Aguas de Pozo*.

Rashida James-Saadiya is a writer, visual artist, and cultural educator. Her work addresses otherness, aesthetics, and the complexities of womanhood in America. In addition, she is a founding member and coeditor of *Voyages*, a quarterly online journal exploring complexities of Africana arts and culture through progressive literature, Afrofuturism, and creative thinking.

Honorée Fanonne Jeffers is the author of the poetry collections *The Glory Gets* (Wesleyan University Press, 2015), *Red Clay Suite* (Southern Illinois University Press, 2007), *Outlandish Blues* (Wesleyan University Press, 2003); and *The Gospel of Barbecue* (The Kent State University Press, 2000), selected by Lucille Clifton for the Stan and Tom Wick Poetry Prize. She has received fellowships from the American Antiquarian Society, the Breadloaf Conference, the National Endowment of the Arts, the Vermont Studio Center, and the Wytter Bynner Foundation through the Library of Congress. She is the Associate Professor and Creative Writing Coordinator at University of Oklahoma.

Ashley M. Jones earned an MFA in Poetry at Florida International University. She was a 2015 Rona Jaffe Writer's Award winner, and her debut collection *Magic City Gospel* is forthcoming from Hub City Press. Her work has been published by the Academy of American Poets, *pluck!*, *PMS: PoemMemoirStory*, and many other journals. She is an editor of *[PANK] Magazine*, and she teaches creative writing at the Alabama School of Fine Arts in Birmingham, Alabama.

Fayaz Kabani has an MFA in Creative Writing and is currently working on his dissertation in Renaissance Literature at the University of South Carolina. He teaches English at Allen University.

Len Lawson is the author of the upcoming chapbook *Before the Night Wakes You* (Finishing Line Press). He has been accepted to the Ph.D. in English Literature and Criticism program at Indiana University of Pennsylvania. Len is a 2015 Pushcart Prize and Best of the Net nominee and a 2016 Callaloo Fellow. His poetry appears or is forthcoming in *Callaloo*, *[PANK]*, *Mississippi Review*, *Pittsburgh Poetry Review*, *Winter Tangerine Review*, and elsewhere. He is a Poetry Reader and Book Reviewer for *Up the Staircase Quarterly* and an English instructor at Central Carolina Technical College.

Scott Murray was born in Scotland and was told as a child that poetry was not for the likes of him. He is a retired religious studies and philosophy teacher.

Kathleen Nalley is the author of *Nesting Doll* and *American Sycamore*. Her poetry has appeared in *New Flash Fiction Review, Slipstream, Rivet, storySouth*, and other journals. Recently, Marjory Wentworth selected one of her poems for the Saluda River Prize for Poetry presented by the Jasper Project. She has an MFA from Converse College and teaches at Clemson University.

Jerlean Noble is a retiree from the University of South Carolina. She is President and Founder of the Columbia Writers Alliance. She has published seven books and co-authored two.

Donald Pardlow, PhD, an Associate Professor of English at Claflin University in Orangeburg, South Carolina, the author of *Field Notes of a Gypsy Scholar* (2014) and co-editor of *Cultivating Visionary Leadership by Learning for Global Success: Beyond the Language and Literature Classroom* (2015).

Pasckie Pascua, a survivor of the Marcos dictatorial regime in his home-country of the Philippines, is a teacher, filmmaker, publisher, artist, and musician. Pasckie has a Communication Arts/Journalism degree from the University of the Philippines' Institute of Mass Communication. He edits the community paper *The Indie*. He is also the founding executive director of Traveling Bonfires. Pasckie's most recent book of poetry and short prose is *Red is the Color of my Night*.

Michele Reese is the author of the poetry collection *Following Phia* (WordTech Editions). Her poems have appeared in the *The Paris Review, Congeries, Blackberry, Smartish Pace*, and other literary journals and anthologies. She is a professor of English at the University of South Carolina-Sumter.

About the Cover

Hands-On: A Community Hand-Casting Project is an interdisciplinary arts project founded in 2017 by Kara Gunter, an artist and educator living and working in Columbia, SC.

In late 2016, Gunter began to wonder how, as an artist, she could help foster empathy and connection in her community. "Though we are living in the most peaceful and prosperous time in human history, in some respects the world seems like a more dangerous and unfriendly place," she says. "In that fear, we are quick to draw lines in the sand, and entrench ourselves within the communities in which we are most comfortable. Traditionally, these would be communities which are most like us in race, class, education level, religion, nationality, political alignment, and so on. How does one encourage folks from such disparate backgrounds to sit down for a spell and learn a bit about each other?"

From this question, Hands-On: A Community Hand-Casting Project was born.

"If I could bring strangers together, from disparate backgrounds, and have them touch for 30 minutes while I cast their hands and have them speak with each other while doing so, then together we would be bridging chasms that may not otherwise be crossed," the artist says.

In January 2017, co-editors of *Hand in Hand: Poets Respond to Race*, Al Black and Len Lawson, met with Gunter for the first casting of the artist's project. Their hands are depicted on the cover of this book.

For more information about Hands-On: A Community Hand-Casting Project visit **handsoncolumbia.wordpress.**

CPSIA information can be obtained
at www.ICGtesting.com
Printed in the USA
FSOW01n1848130218
44317FS